Stars and Galaxies

Looking Beyond the Solar System

This book introduces children to the elements that are the farthest away in the universe, as well as the least known: stars, constellations, black holes, galaxies, and so on, by means of old legends and modern scientific astronomy. The book also suggests an interesting practical activity for parents or teachers to do with the children, which is followed by helpful teaching guidelines.

English translation of *Stars and Galaxies*
©Copyright 1998 by Barron's Educational Series, Inc.

©Copyright TREVOL PRODUCCIONS EDITORIALS S.C.P., 1998. Barcelona, Spain.

Original title of the book in Catalan: *Estrelles i galàxies; més enllà del Sistema Solar.*

Address all inquiries to:
Barron's Educational Series, Inc.
250 Wireless Boulevard
Hauppauge, New York 11788
http://www.barronseduc.com

International Standard Book Number 0-7641-0686-4
Library of Congress Catalog Card Number 98-73389

Printed in Spain

98765432

Stars and Galaxies

Looking Beyond the Solar System

Text: Miquel Pérez   Illustrations: Maria Rius

BARRON'S

Our friends have found an old book of legends in their grandparents' attic.... A long, long time ago, in the high mountains of a far away country, there was a young shepherd who looked after his sheep day and night.

The shepherd often watched the sky at night and he could see a lot of tiny spots of light. He had always known that they were stars. He knew their names and could find his way in the dark, guided by the North Star. But he had so many questions about the stars that one day he decided to go and find the wise Knowitall.

Today, we know the exact positions of many stars. We have them classified by name, size, age, and type.

Knowing the constellations formed by the stars in the Northern and Southern Hemispheres is helpful when we need to find our way outside in the dark.

Searching for Knowitall, the shepherd and his dog walked for many days and many nights until they reached the sea. An old fisherman, who knew the sky well, told them: "The stars you see at night are balls of fire like our sun, but they are so far away that we see them as tiny spots of light. If you look carefully, you will see that some are blue and others are red, yellow, or white."

Today we know that the color of a star depends on its temperature, age, and size. Stars originate from revolving clouds of gas. Sometimes, one of these clouds condenses and starts to burn, thus creating a star.

After a long walk, the shepherd and his dog arrived at a town. There was a man in the town who spoke about stars and explained he had seen a star explode and disappear in the dark of the night.

We now know that, after millions of years releasing light and heat, some stars grow colder and smaller until they are extinguished. But a very big star can explode instead of growing cold.

This explosion forms a supernova. With the passage of time it can become a black hole, which is considered to be a collapsed star absorbing its own rays and so becoming invisible.

The shepherd kept on walking until he finally arrived at a small village. A very old woman stopped him and asked:

"Where are you going in such a hurry?"

"I am going to see a wise man so he can tell me about the stars."

The old woman said:

"If you want, I can tell you something too. Look at the sky on a clear night and you will see a long whitish band that crosses it. That is the Milky Way."

If astronomers could travel now over the Milky Way, they would see something like this.

The Milky Way is our galaxy. Like many others, it is a huge system that comprises all the stars we can see at first sight, as well as the sun and its planets. The Earth and the rest of the solar system are toward one end of this gigantic conglomerate of stars.

The shepherd met some countryfolk who offered to put him up for the night because he looked very tired. While they were having some supper, the farmers told him that, according to a legend, the Milky Way originated when the Greek goddess Hera was breast-feeding Heracles and some drops of milk fell from the baby's mouth.

The latest theories by astronomers claim that the Milky Way originated about 15 billion years ago from the accumulation of large quantities of gas and

dust projected into space by a huge explosion called the Big Bang, which was the origin of the entire universe.

After his long trip, the shepherd reached the house of the wise man called Knowitall.

"Where are you coming from?" asked the wise man.

"We have come a long way to ask you to tell us everything about the stars. But on my way here I have learned a lot of things, such as the story about the Milky Way, the origin of the stars, and their colors."

The wise man was very surprised and said:

"You know almost as much as I do, but since you are so interested, I will show you a wonderful and useful instrument."

Nowadays, astronomers observe the sky through big telescopes. Many are located on top of mountains, where the atmosphere is thinner and there are no city lights. Thanks to telescopes, astronomers can see galaxies and millions of stars.

Our friends were happy to know so many new things and waited eagerly for the night, when they could contemplate the magnificent spectacle of the sky, like the shepherd did when he was looking after his sheep.

Teaching Activities

The best conditions to watch the sky at night are: a dark, clear night, no clouds or moon, and a location far from city lights. Any time of the year is good, although there is usually better visibility in August and December. However, it gets dark very late in summer, and in winter it is uncomfortable to stay out at night because of the cold. We recommend warm clothes, a compass for beginners, and a blanket to make the activity comfortable and enjoyable.

1

After sitting down in the chosen location and waiting for our eyes to grow used to the darkness, we will be impressed by the number of stars we can see; only some of them can be seen all year. The Earth rotates on its axis and revolves around the sun, thus creating the changes in the stellar landscape.

We, the inhabitants of the Northern Hemisphere, are fortunate to have a star that always indicates the north, which we call the North Star. It is not a star of the first magnitude and you need to be patient to locate it, so follow these instructions: First find Ursa Major, or the Great Bear, toward the north. According to the time of year, the Big Dipper of the Great Bear can appear in different places, but it is a group of very bright stars (see Figure 2). You can use its stars α and ß as a reference. Multiply the distance between them five times and you will find the North Star. The revolving axis of the Earth points toward the North Star, so, as the night goes on, we can see all stars moving around it (see Figure 3).

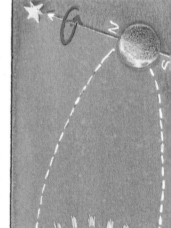

2

In low latitudes, as in the South of the United States, the Great Bear may be under the horizon in the fall and winter. In that case, it is better to look for the W-shape of Cassiopeia toward the north, but remember it also has very bright stars and it can appear to be in different places. It does not indicate the way to the North Star as accurately as the Great Bear, but it helps.

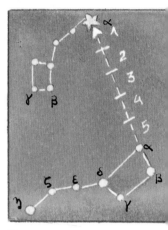

Once we have the North Star, we can see the constellation to which it belongs, called Ursa Minor, or Little Bear, with stars of a very low magnitude except ß and γ. In the Great Bear we can see the star ζ, called Mizar, that has another star close to it, called Alcor. The Arabs, from whom we have inherited most of the names of the stars, used it to test the sight of their future warriors; those who could spot Alcor had sharp eyes and were able to do battle.

After recognizing the constellations of the Great Bear and the Little Bear with the North Star and Cassiopeia, depending on the time of the year we can watch different things.

• If it is winter, at approximately 9:00 p.m. Universal Time (U.T.) in December, January, or February, we can look toward the south and find Orion (see Figure 4). Orion is a giant in Greek mythology and in the constellation he is depicted with a sword in his left hand. The belt is formed by three stars. Following them toward the east we will find Sirius, a bluish star and the brightest in the heavens. Toward the west, we will find Aldebaran in Taurus, and above it, there is the cluster of stars called the Pleiades. Betelgeuse and Rigel are interesting stars in Orion. The latter means "foot" and it is a supergiant[1], which is 1,400 light-years away[2] and 50,000 times brighter than the sun. The big Orion Nebula (M 42) is one of the few that can be seen with the naked eye; with binoculars, it is a stirring sight.

• If it is spring, at approximately 10:00 p.m. U.T. in March, April, or May, we can see Leo by looking south (see Figure 5). As the name indicates, it represents a lion that resembles the Egyptian sphinx. Toward the north, if we put together stars η, ζ, and ε in the Great Bear, we will form a curve that points to Arcturus (see Figure 8), a yellowish or orange star that represents the bear-keeper.

• If it is summer, at approximately 11:00 p.m. U.T. in June, July, or August, we can see directly over our heads (that is, at the zenith) the so-called Summer Triangle (see Figure 6), formed by Deneb in the Cygnus Constellation, Vega in Lyra, and Altair in Aquila. Through the center of the triangle we can see the Milky Way[3], the luminous whitish band that crosses the sky from end to end over our heads. We will have to

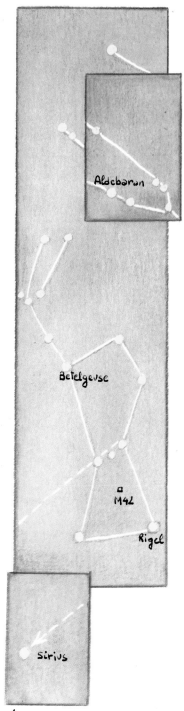

4

[1]See explanations No. 2 and 2.2 in Teaching Guidelines
[2]See explanation No. 1 in Teaching Guidelines
[3]See explanation No. 3 in Teaching Guidelines

be a little patient to see it, as its luminosity is quite low. Next to Deneb ("tail" in Arabic, tail of the cygnet or swan, of course) we can see a giant cloud called the North American Nebula because of its shape as seen with a telescope. In the Cygnus Constellation there is also Cygnius X-1, a supposed black hole[4] that cannot be seen, obviously.

• If it is fall, at approximately 10:00 p.m. U.T. in September, October, or November, watching between the south and the zenith, we can try to see Pegasus (see Figure 7), named after the mythical winged horse. Its stars are not many but the big square, known as the Great Square of Pegasus, is easy to distinguish. Finally, Pegasus marks the start of the Andromeda Constellation, famous because of the Andromeda Galaxy it contains. It is one of the few elements outside our galaxy that we can observe with the naked eye. It is a spiral resembling the Milky Way, with two hundred billion suns plus dust and gas.

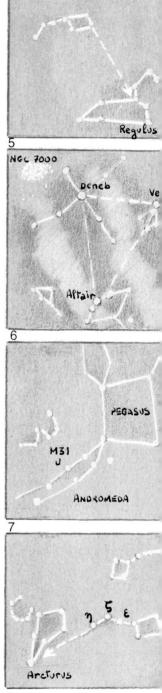

5

6

7

8

---

[4]See explanation No. 2 and 2.3 in Teaching Guidelines

Teaching Guidelines

1. Stars are huge balls of fire that are very far away. The closest to us is Proxima Centauri, which is four light years away, meaning that the light it radiates takes four years to reach us. This means that what we now see on Proxima Centauri happened four years ago. Light travels at a speed of 186,000 miles per second; for example, the light from the sun needs about eight and a half minutes to reach the Earth.

2. The origin of the stars, like that of planets and galaxies, is in the force of attraction of the particles that clump together to form numerous clouds of gas and dust in our galaxy. After millions of years, these particles condense, making a dense mass with more and more gravitational force that attracts more and more particles.

   There is a time when this gravitational force is so powerful that the particles forming the mass (mostly hydrogen atoms) collide at such a speed that they become different particles (four atoms of hydrogen make an atom of helium) and release an enormous amount of energy in the form of light and heat, as well as X and gamma rays. The cloud has now become a star. Its mass determines the duration of the balance between the gravitational force, which keeps all the particles together, and the interaction of the particles, a nuclear fusion process, which tends to impel them outward (see Figure 9).

2.1 If a condensed cloud is very small, it may never become a star (the nuclear fusion never starts), and it may form a planet. The smallest stars, called red dwarfs, use up their fuel very slowly and last longer than other stars.

2.2 If the star is medium sized, like our sun, it can keep the balance of gravity and nuclear fusion and release light and heat for millions of years until its fuel is exhausted. It can then go through the following process: First, it can expand to become a red giant or a supergiant, and later, it can shrink until it becomes a small white star that grows colder and colder until it is extinguished.

2.3 If the star is very big, its evolution will be similar to that of the sun except in the last phases. These supergiant stars can

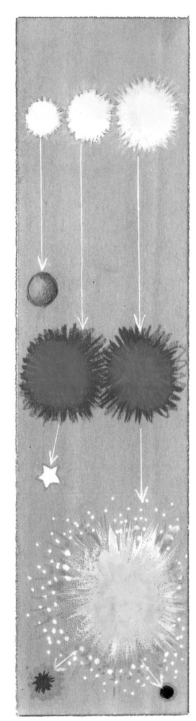

not keep a steady balance very long and they tend to explode (supernova), releasing a lot of light. Afterwards, they can go in one of two ways:

- They can become extremely dense neutron stars rotating very fast and giving off radio waves at regular intervals, like a lighthouse. We call these stars pulsars.
- They can become black holes if they are denser than pulsars. The density of any black hole is so big that the gravitational force does not let the rays of light be released.

3. The Milky Way (see Figure 10) is the name that was given by Romans and Greeks to the luminous band that crosses the sky. This band and our galaxy have the same name, because they are the same. This band is how we see the center of our galaxy in profile from the Earth. The stars on either side of the band—the ones we usually know—are those that are somewhat separated from the center of the galaxy. The Milky Way is a huge conglomerate of stars, gases, and dust that, together with some thirty other galaxies, form our galactic cluster, known as a Local Group (see Figure 11), one of the many clusters that form the universe. The Milky Way is a spiral that looks like a disk with four arms around it. Near the end of one of these arms is the sun and, obviously, the Earth. We may wonder why the luminosity of this band is so weak if it is the center of the galaxy. The reason is that the enormous amount of cosmic dust floating among the stars makes visibility poor.

Now we know the postal address of our planet, just in case we need to get mail from an extraterrestrial creature.

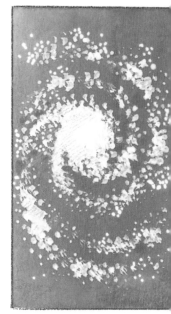

10

11

INTERGALACTIC MAIL

_____(Name)

_____(Street, city, country)

*The Earth - Solar System*_____(Planet - Planetary System)

*Milky Way*_____(Galaxy)

*Local Group*_____(Group or galactic cluster)

*Universe*_____